The Ember Ever There

poems on change, grief, growth
recovery, and rediscovery

Jean McCarthy

ISBN: 978-1-9992999-2-7 (paperback)
ISBN: 978-1-9992999-3-4 (ebook)

BEGINNING

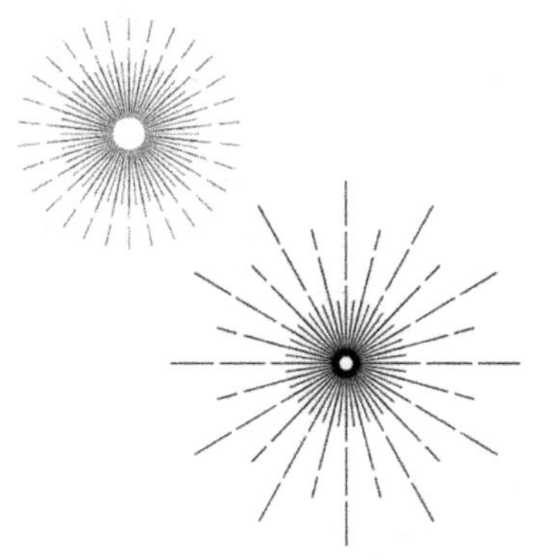

BEGIN

begin
with the choice
to live
fully
freely

unafraid
to show up
such as
you
are

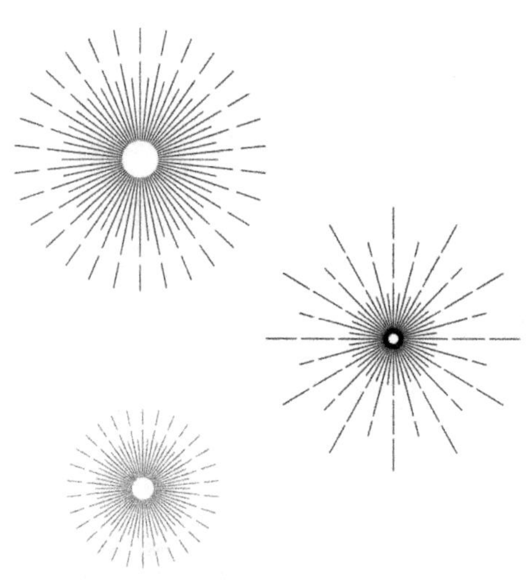

THE EMBER EVER THERE

oh, my soul
that glorious thing
radiant
despite me

the ember ever there

even as
I cried out
lies of shame
to hide and muddy
my truth

I felt certain
it was gone
but through the years
it glowed unknown
under layers of
scars and secrets

sapphire light
steady and strong
shines
on and on
indifferent
to matters of surface

truth awaiting
rediscovery

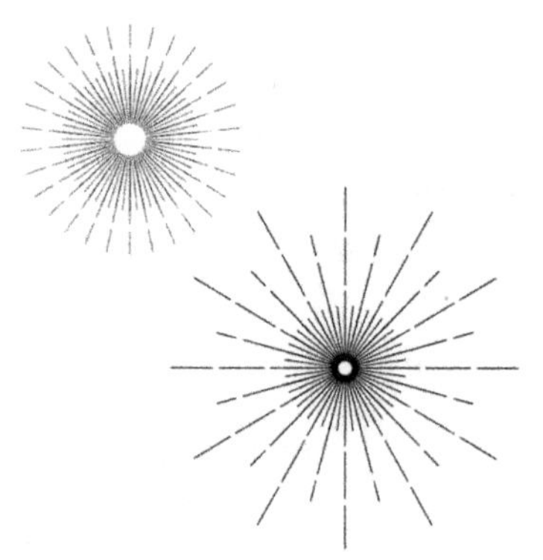

WHY NOW?

Do not ask
Why now?

When the
better question
is

How could I live
another moment
separated
from
myself?

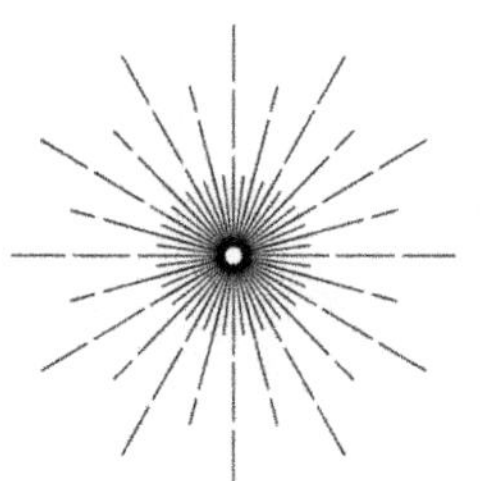

MORNING

I watch
this newborn day
unfold
and promise myself
I won't ask too much of it

after all
it's just a day

I won't expect
to change the world
or even myself today
but
only nudge
us both
in a better direction

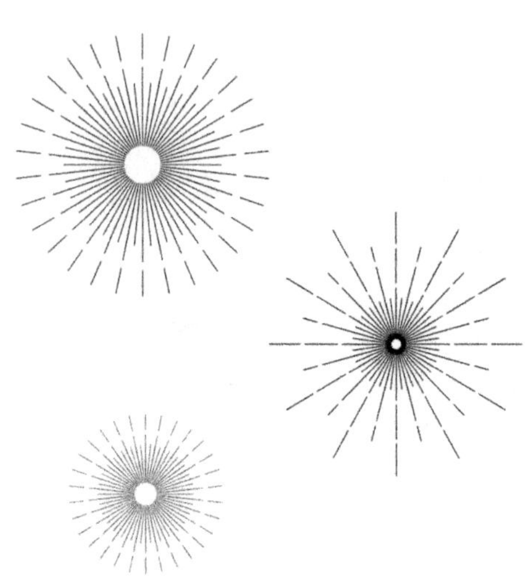

SUPPOSING

suppose
I kept
all the good
and let you go

suppose
I stood up
hand on heart
and owned my ground

suppose
your reassurances and whispers
were never true

what if I'm
powerful
capable
deserving

then
now is the time

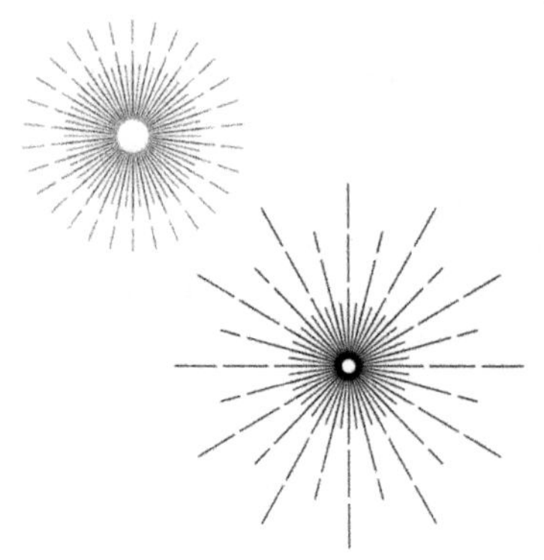

DREAMS

No dream is
complete
until
the moment
of waking
when
reality
unveils
the vision

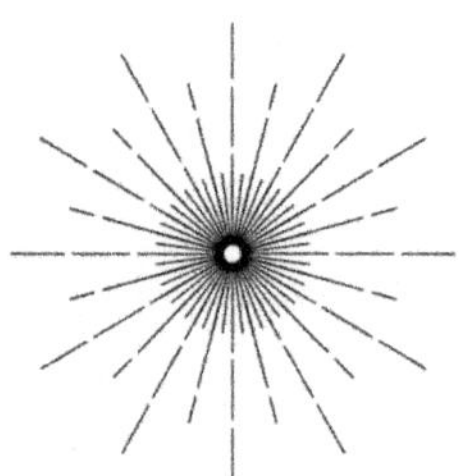

MOUNTAIN POSE

standing tall
head high
mountain pose

claiming space
owning truth

here I am
fully in my
power

wise
strong
here
I am

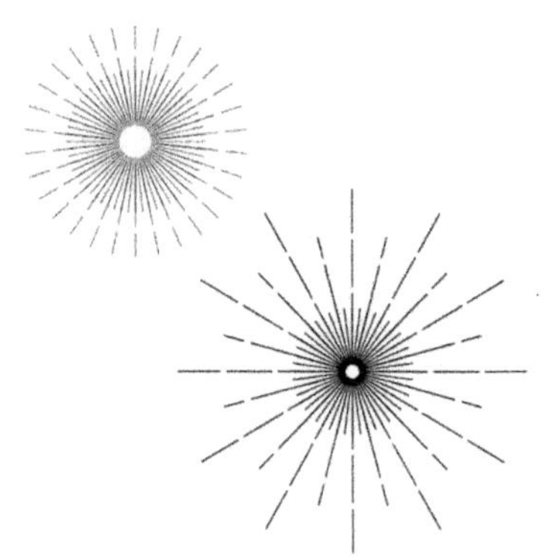

ADRIFT

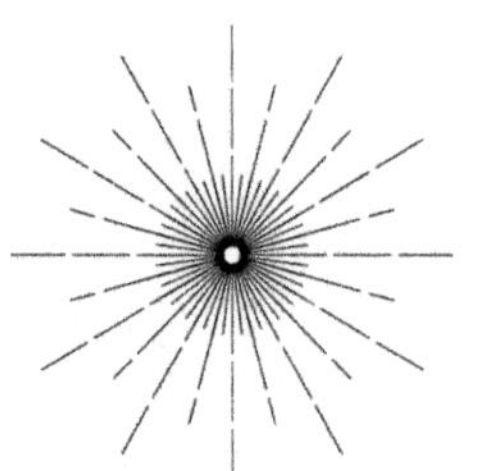

OBEDIENCE

Voices inside
call obvious lies
I choose to believe

You deserve it
You've earned it
You need it
You're broken

Voices inside
Call me by name
Saying 'you'
Never 'I'
And I listen to others
I do as I'm told

Fooling myself
With ventriloquist skills
Rigid lips
Feed the need

Guidance
(Even in the wrong direction)
Renders me blameless
The voices said 'you'
So I listened
I always listen
Like such a
Good Girl

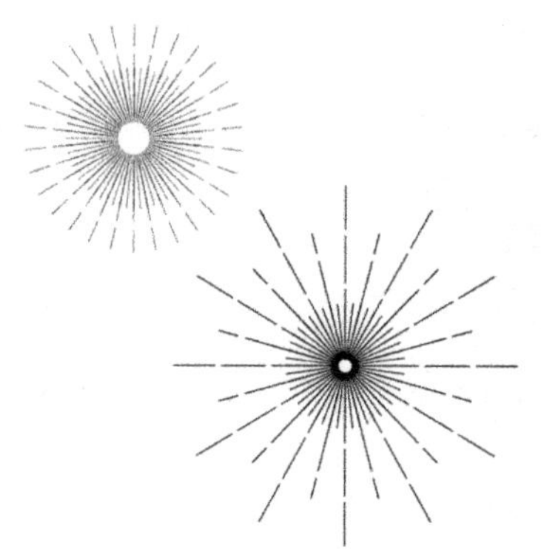

SLEEPLESS

Heart races
Tears flow
Wide awake
Reason goes

Thoughts loop
Memories roll
Hours pass
Panic's toll

Sleep evades
Let go
Look inside
Brave soul

Stare down
Source unknown
Tend wounds
Not alone

Morning comes
Sunrise glows
Arise arise
Move slow

Mirrored face
Reflection shows
Daylight truth
Healing grows

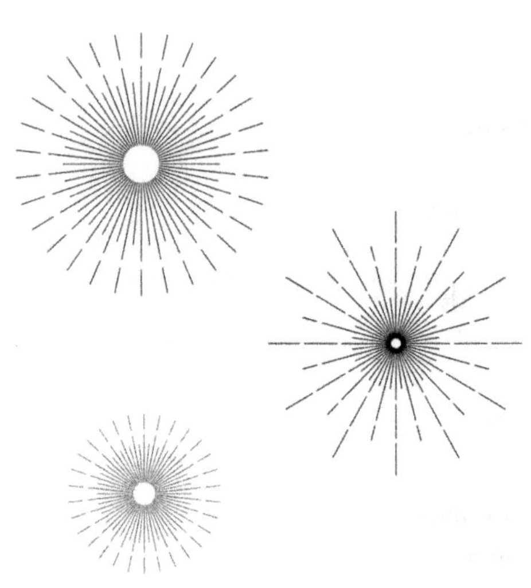

PARTS

Which mask
is required
to convince you
I'm worth your while
in charge
in need
independent
entwined

Tell me
exactly
who I'm to be

Custom moulded

Contorted to fit

Exchanges or returns
Will not be permitted

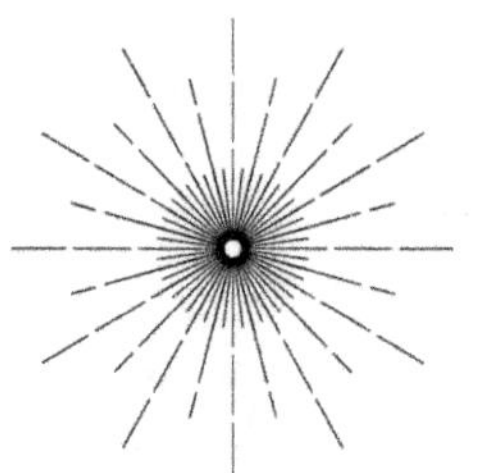

THE GIRL INSIDE

Stay hidden,
I said, to the girl inside
How can I keep you safe
if you laugh so loudly in a crowd?
How can I make them like you
if you shine in their eyes?
How can we fit in this small space
I've been given
if your bigness is on display?
Stay hidden, I said,
it's for your your own good
You can't go around
with your heart blazing heat
The moths will come at us
and so will the cold souls
hands out like zombies seeking warmth
wanting more
always more
It's too much to bear
Stay hidden
Stay safe

———

Her mouth moves
but the words are not ours
Stay safe, says a voice,
deep and dark from the past
while her eyes plead
rescue me
She begs me to save her

as she locks me away
but morning sun softens
the bars of my prison
a crack in her armour
a chance
to kick down the wall
she's erected between us
I'm coming for you
Hold up a mirror
we are one and the same
Her unconvincing lip-sync
a beat behind
like an old kung fu movie
Together we'll run
Thunderous steps
Freedom in motion
Precision itself
Desperate for
Unity

LOSS AND GRIEF

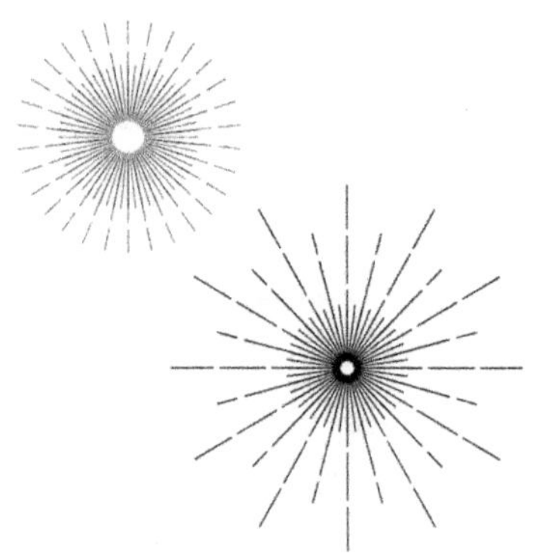

FAREWELL

You've gone
I'm not sorry
I've locked the door
Still I
Ache
Cry
Pace

Alone

Grief
So unexpected
Fills the void
Heavy dark morose
Unwelcome
Necessary

Bargains considered
Rejected

Shoulders back
Awaiting peace

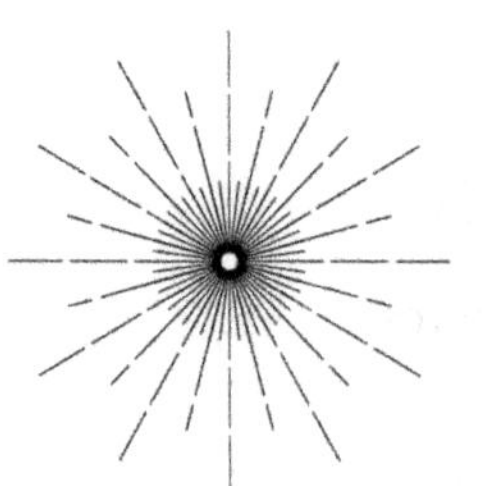

PERSPECTIVE

I stopped wondering
How could you?

And started thinking
Why would you?

Which led me to wonder
If you even knew yourself

Perhaps you were all instinct
Oblivious to the outcome
Just doing what came naturally

Because humans have patterns
And you're not so different
Than anyone else.

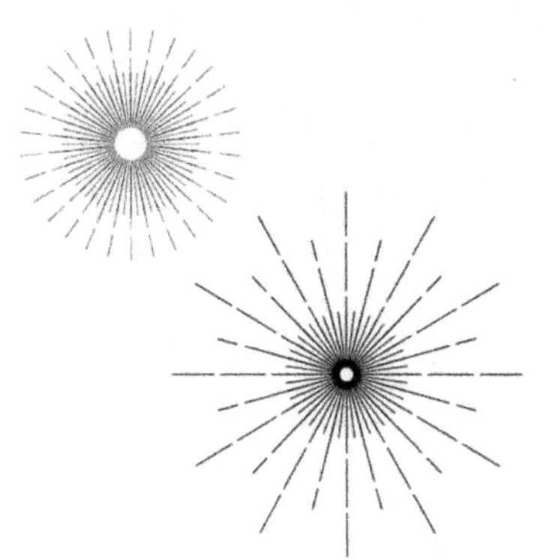

REACTION

You recoil
as if
burnt
by the changes
embodied
in a posture
of power
and a mind
at peace

My solace repels
My strength offends

I've broken the contract
signed in my sleep
that bound me
to bend
and betray
myself

No more

Your story depends
on my compliance
and without it
you descend
into
vile
vertigo

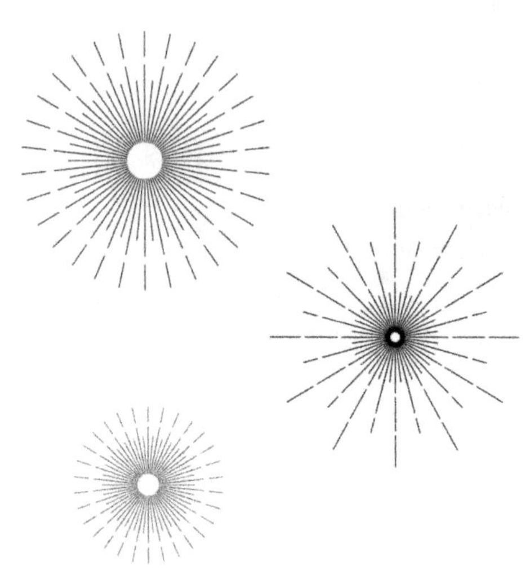

GRIEF

Grief
The night
I cannot weep
Feel nothing if at all
Time
Goes by
I cannot sleep
Memories weave and call

Hold me
Gently
Never cease
Whisper that you're near
Send me
Subtle signs of peace
Til I believe you're here

Dismiss
The angry
Words I speak
We both know
They're not true
Know
The pain
You caused in life
And with your passing, too

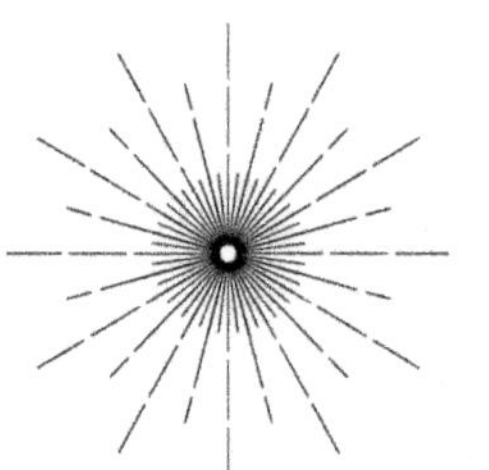

LONGING

Oh, to take your hand again
And walk through parts unknown
Oh, to sit down next to you
And feel as if at home

Oh, to hear your laughter
And know it's just for me
I ache to feel the comfort
Of your easy company

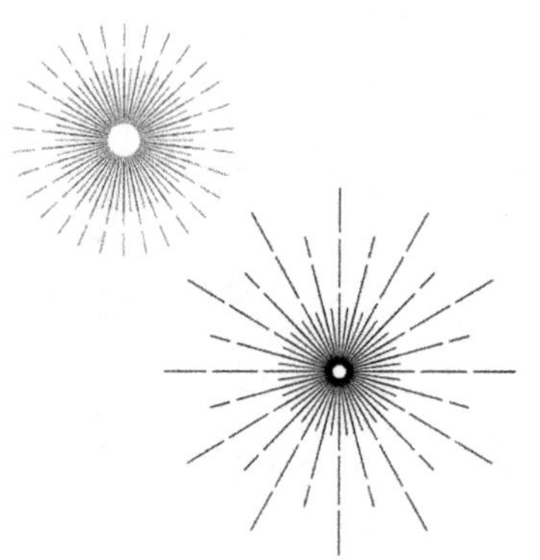

LOST

I cannot feel
your quiet
light

where have you gone?

perhaps
I am
the
lost one

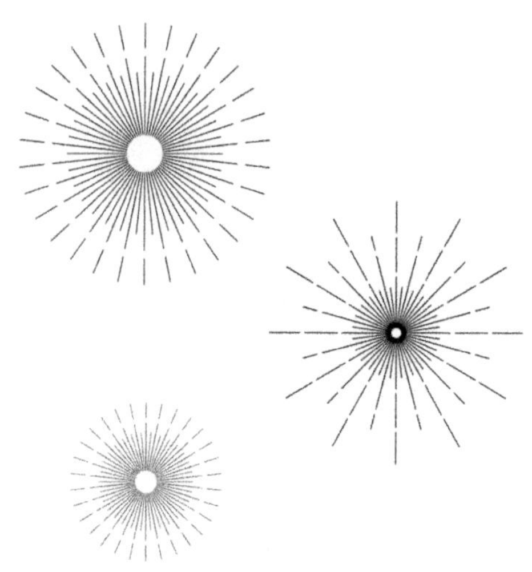

HEALING

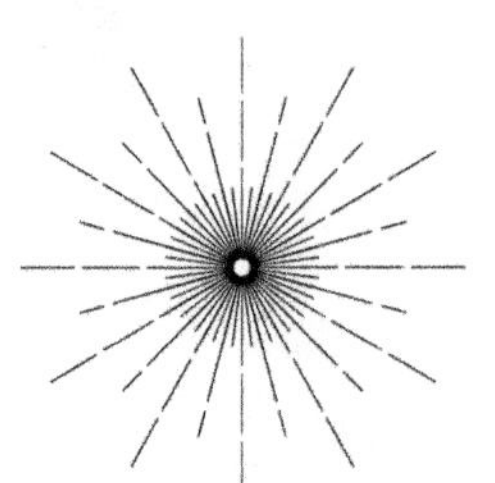

SUNRISE

and just like that
when hope felt lost
the sunrise
lit the mountaintop
insisting
we all
look up

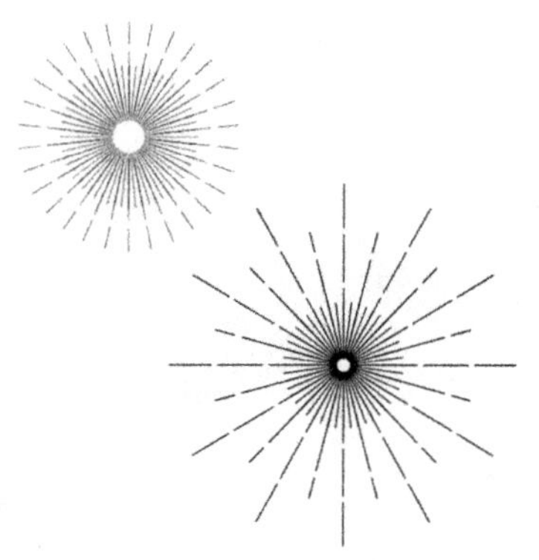

I AM HER

So this is the woman
I've waited a lifetime to see

This is how
the face will
soften

This is how
the shape will
round

This is how
the grey will
appear

This is how
the arms will
hold

This is how
the words will
ring

This is how
the heart will
shine

Finally
Finally
I am her

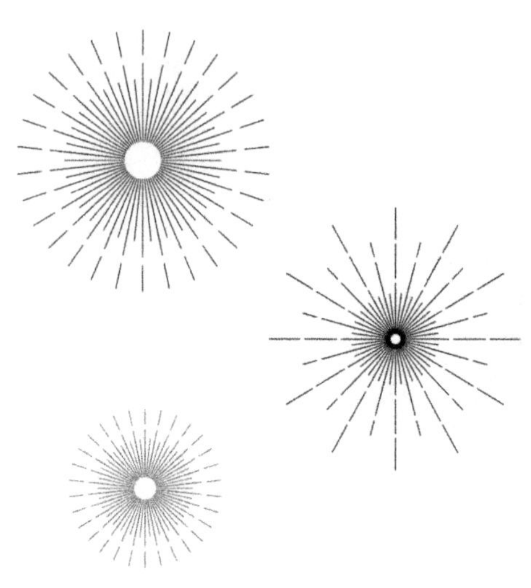

SPARKS

the sparks
from my heart
long perceived as problematic
as harbingers of doom
or needless worry
were never to be feared

they were friendly all along

a tap
not a hammer

a bell
not an alarm

asking for my notice

whispers of truth
in a language
I forgot
I'd ever known

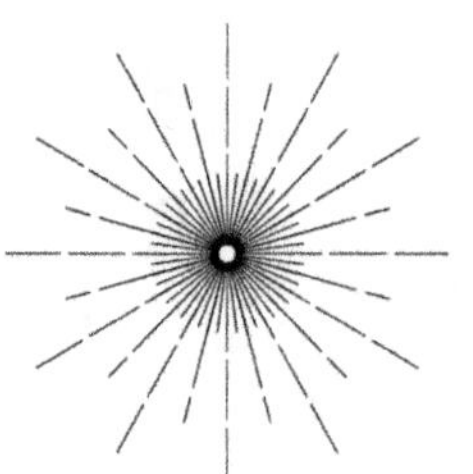

THE EVENT

Resurrect
The girl inside
who knows how to
sparkle
Spin her once around the room
A glittering tour of duty
Oh, she is good

Nice to see you
Yes, yes
Of course
We must
Wonderful
***WON**derful*

A champion sprinter
can still be
terrible
at marathons

Usher her out
Thank her for coming
Wrap her in flannel
and tuck her in bed

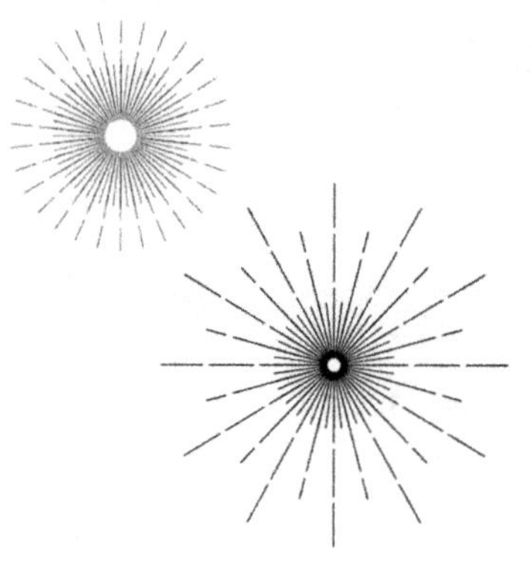

TRUTH

a truth emerged
suddenly there
filling an invisible void
with utter understanding

took the place of
unexpressed
disappointment
lack
resentment

shifted with a click of alignment

relief from
discomfort disguised as personality

it cannot be unknown
this truth
this insight
this wisdom

and who would surrender peace once given?

tucked into a pocket
a guarded treasure
touched for reassurance
it is mine
it found me
I am grateful

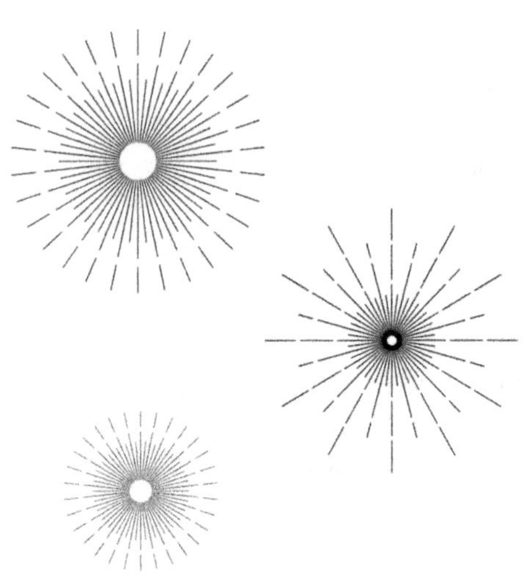

A WAVERING TUNE

whistle softly
a wavering tune
that flounders like
my thoughts
my will
my opinion of myself
not so strong
and yet
meant to be
heard

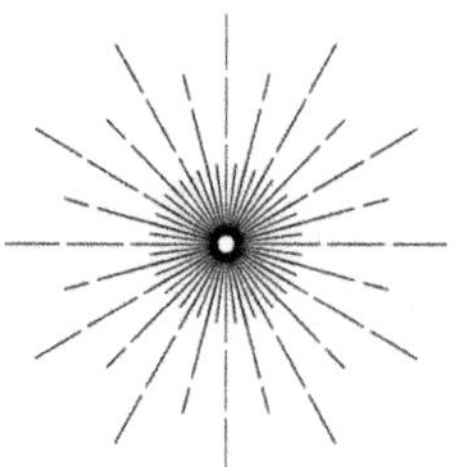

UNDER THE SKY

When trouble consumes
Problems abound
Looping thoughts repeat

Stand under the sky
Until it is clear

We are small
And so are our worries

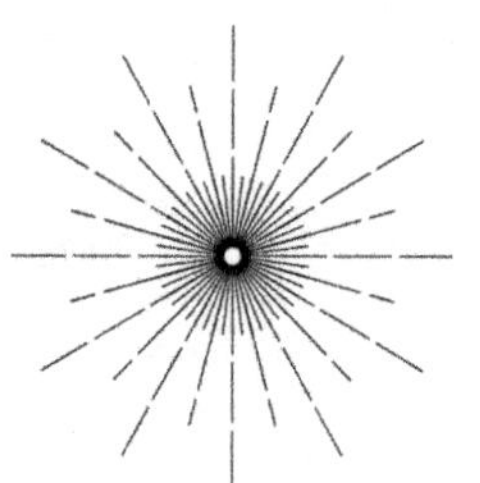

MORNING PAGES

such delight
to fill a page
to sharpen a pencil down to a nub
to be mid-word when a pen runs dry

such relief
to have written so much
as to exhaust resources
and to have spared others
from hearing half-baked
thoughts
fears
and dreams
left on paper
instead
to finish forming

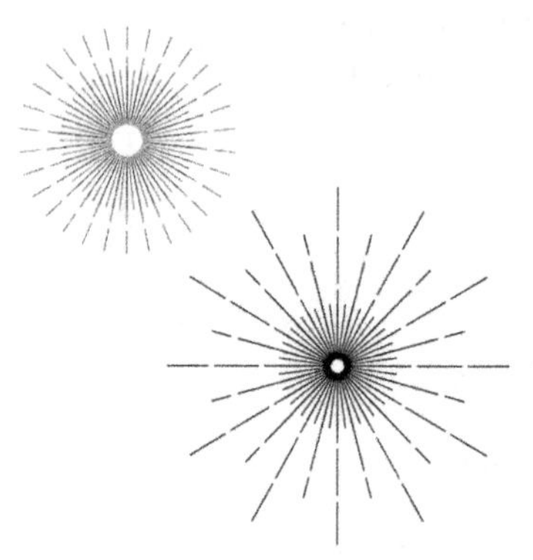

SLIPPERY

Hold me not
to versions of yesterday

Do not pin me to the past

Grab my collar
and I'll slip from the sleeves
to leave you holding
my garment
like a shed skin

Love me where I am today
but search for me tomorrow

Do not assume
you'll find me here
curled in shame
anchored in pain
I plan to move on
ever forward
ever onward
ever better
always trying
growing
healing
reaching
until
I finally
fade
away

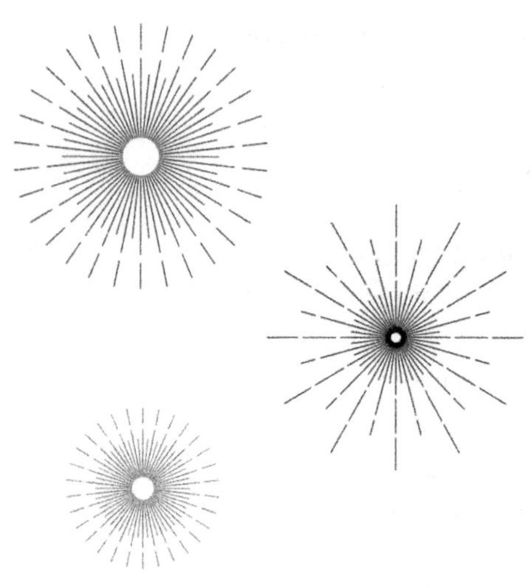

NORTH

North calls me away
From the softness of South
Away from the easy
Away from the known
From the common
And comfortable

I don't want to want it
Yet wish to want more

North Star
Guidance
Steady and sure

North winds
Refreshment
Sips of cool truth

Northern lights
Joyful
A dance of abandon

Wholeheartedly hard
Pragmatic
Meaningful

All that life is meant to be

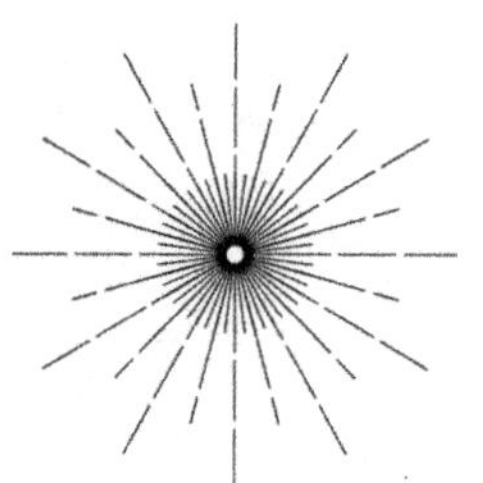

REFLECTIONS ON STEPS

The First Step
of a Twelve Step
program of recovery
is to accept powerlessness
over one's numbing mechanism of choice.

POWERLESSNESS

Powerless?
No.
It's there somewhere.
I swear.

Powerless?
Yes.
In some ways,
I guess.

Powerless?
Really?
May I skip this one?
I just want to be done.

Powerless.
Why?

To release the weight
Hands weren't meant to carry
And free the heart
For better tasks.

The Second Step
is to acknowledge
that some power
greater than oneself exists
and can restore healing and order.

A HIGHER POWER

Of course there's something
greater than me;
new leaves bloom,
mountains tower.
It's there.
I see.
Yes, the universe
is beyond my scope.
My world's gotten small,
I'm cramped inside.
I can't
Locate hope.
You say I can choose
the source of this power;
the departed
or revered,
my favourite flower.
I want to debate this
Argue or rant:
You're wrong.
This is stupid.
I won't.
I can't.
Then comes awakening
from within or without.
I see it.
I feel it.
I never had doubt.

The Third Step
is to turn one's life
over to that greater power.

SURRENDER

Take it.
Oh, wait.
I'd like it back,
Just for a moment
While I adjust this
And add to that.
Take it.
Oh now, hey,
I'm telling my story
And need it for demonstration.
I'll just...
Here.
Alright then, go ahead.
Yes, that's better.
Thanks.
But...
One more thing.
Well, it's mine, you see.
It's who I am.
It's what I
DO.
So I'll keep it with me
And let you know if I need help.
That won't work?
Will you at least hold it where I can see it?
I don't approve of
unattended baggage.

The Fourth Step
is to list out all of one's burdensome
secrets, regrets, resentments,
and other points of shame.

INVENTORY

Pages and pages
I cannot stop
It just keeps coming

Dot after dot
I've never connected before

Oh God
It's worse than I thought
But it feels so good
And oh wait, there's more.

Just write
Don't stop don't think don't edit
Just write it all
Until it's done
Writing itself

I'll have to share this in the next step
No, don't think about that
Just write
Get it out
And then and then and then
And I...
And I...
Plus also
And so
Then I
But he
So I
And she

But I
And so and so and so
Next I
So I
Then they
Until
But then
It just
I did
I was
I went
I offered
I tried
I didn't
I should have
But I
Then
And then
And so
And I
And then
And that's all.
I swear.
Except...
Oh, and also
I guess
I did
Until
And then
Again.
But well
They
I
We
Did

Didn't
Again
Again
Should have
Didn't
Could have
Wouldn't
So I
Then they
But really

It's all true.

That's it.
That's really it.

For now.

The Fifth Step
involves taking ownership of
wrong doings and imperfections
uncovered in the previous step
by admitting them to oneself,
to the greater power,
and to another person.

SPILLING

Spill out your truth
to someone who will not blink,
turn,
tsk,
or run,
Who'll stay til you're done.

Give voice to your past.
It can't reappear,
won't rehappen
or burn.
It will lessen in turn.

Give it air, let it breathe.
Stare it down.
Set it loose.
Let it be
Til you're finally free.

The Sixth Step
is to become ready
to have these soft spots removed
by the greater power.

READINESS

Standing
in naked honesty

Ready to release
Ready to renew

Eager to learn
how to live in a world
where old beliefs
are but food for thought
and the contract is always up
for renegotiation

The Seventh Step
is to ask for the old ways
to be removed and replaced
with better practices and principles.

BETTER WAYS

Knee-jerk
self-defensive
barbs and lures
are apparently a choice.

Supposedly, other ways exist.

It's said that one can simply

wait

for a better response
to be delivered
by divine download.

A superior operating system
is on the other side
of the tortuous pause
(if the sound of one's own breathing
can be endured
for seven seconds or so).

Some say it helps to blink.
Others confess to grinning madly
in their confidence of the outcome.

In the notorious
Eighth Step,
a list is made of all persons harmed,
to whom one must become willing
to make amends.

THE LIST

I see now
this list contains
many people I was
SURE
had wounded me.
On reflection
I played a role
I'm now able to own
without defence.

I see now
that
NO ONE KNOWS
does not make anything unimportant;
first because it *happened*
and also
I KNOW
and I'm not no one.

I see now
this list is longer than expected.
It gets easier as I go.
I've unlocked something.

I see now.

The Ninth Step
is to make amends to others,
either directly or indirectly.

AMENDS

Some will look away.
Some will shrug it off.
Some will refuse to grant forgiveness
or even hear the other side,
clinging to their version
because it defines them.

Allow it.
Their reaction is not the point.

Some will finish your sentences,
nod eagerly
and rejoice in the validation
of their perspective,
happier for themselves
than for you.

Accept it.
Their compassion is not your pursuit.

Some will never know that
you've made it right,
corrected course,
mended what you could.

But you'll know
and that's enough.

Others will listen and receive.
The clouds will not part

You may feel nothing
but it will be done.

That's all that matters.

Sidebar I

Inner critic on high alert!
Cue mocking voices in head:
What gives you
the right
to write
poems
about steps?
How dare you
think thoughts,
assign them words
and share them.
Who do you think you are?

The Tenth Step
is to continue the process
of working the steps.

REVEAL AND REPEAT

Healing happens
Bit by bit
Edges soften and lift

raw
and
tender
flesh
below
exposed
soaks in sunshine and fresh, crisp air

Dance around in this new skin
Stretch and reach
Try the limits
See what it can do
Caress it
Slather it with fragrant oil
Live in it fully
As it strengthens and sparkles
Protecting the rest until it's time

and then
bows
and
fades
to opacity
as something better
emerges
from
beneath

its
surface

This is growth that need never end

Even the crone may hide
Spirited renewal
Behind milky eyes
And open her heart
To turn within
Again and again
Exploring with curiosity
Every pattern and outcome

Willing to change
Despite settling bones
Speckled skin and
A world content
to
just
let
her
be.

Sidebar II

Higher self responds to inner critic:
Thanks for showing up.
I know you worry about me
and have my best interest at heart.
Everyone has the right
to think thoughts and share them.
Don't be afraid.
These pages are safe.

The Eleventh Step
is to continually pray and meditate
for direction and purpose
from the greater power

THE ARRANGEMENT

Here's the deal:

You keep exposing
my soft spots
and I'll keep
tending them.

You keep revealing
lessons
and I'll keep
an open heart.

You keep on
running the show
and I'll keep
thanking you.

You keep sending
opportunities
and I'll keep saying
Yes.

The Twelfth Step
is to shine the light of this experience for others
and to use the principles of the process
in all affairs.

THE CYCLE

The outstretched hand
met with a firm grip
pulled to safety
held for warmth
patted for assurance
clasped in friendship
and raised in victory
is eventually
extended
to help another reaching out
and will
pull
hold
pat
clasp
and
be raised
in turn

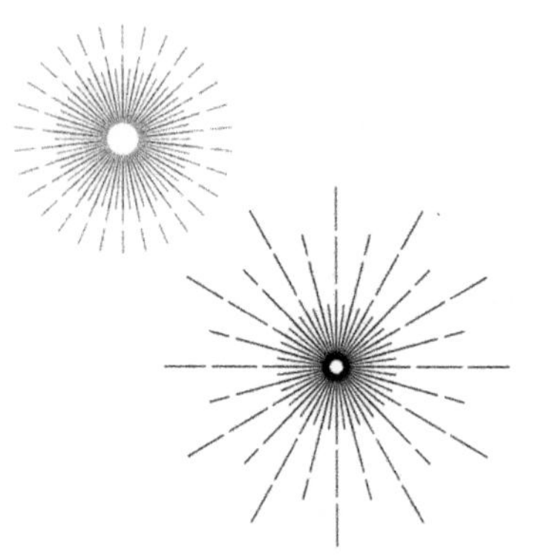

CONNECTIONS

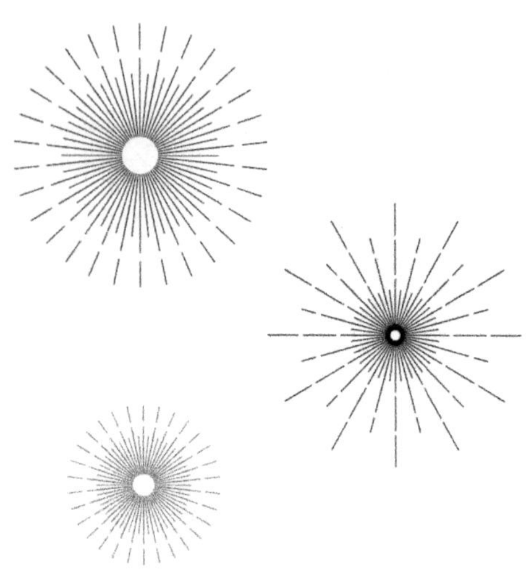

CHAIRS IN A CIRCLE

My dear recovery friends,

I have been waiting for you
and you, it seems,
have been waiting for me, too.

We've stepped into a place
in each other's lives
to fill in an invisible gap,
a void unknown before.

We soothe an unrecognized irritation,
like the noise that goes unnoticed
until it stops
and then suddenly,
ahhhh,
that is better.

Until we found this gap,
this secret zone,
we spent our lives filling in
the obvious slots;
the places reserved for
parents and siblings
and friends and neighbours,
for lovers and children,
for teachers and baristas and gynecologists.
Our accountants know every penny.
Our hairdressers see grey roots
at the napes of our necks
we can never reach on our own.

We thought our lives were full
because all the spaces
were filled.
What more could we possibly need?
All of the bases were covered.

And then.
Then.
We found ourselves in a new place,
a place we came to heal ourselves,
and found each other.

We see ourselves in every person here,
gathered for the same purpose.
Here to restore.
Here to reveal.

We learn this thing called
holding space.
And harder still,
we learn to be held.

We've met in the grey area
we didn't know existed,
a place between
ourselves and the world.
Our circle has capacity
for stunning revelation,
a BS-free zone
that welcomes brutal honesty
and forgives imperfections
yet it does not require
regular lunch dates,
invitations to our children's weddings
or obligatory niceties

other close relationships demand.

(Sure, you'd take the afternoon off
to meet for coffee if I asked,
maybe even offer me
your spare room for the night,
and yet you'd never be offended
if I was nearby and didn't call.)

Some days,
back in the land of black and white,
when life is a grind
and those around me assume I'm just fine,
I might wonder if I imagined you.

Did this time really happen?
Did I sit in the circle and confess
that thing
never acknowledged elsewhere?

I will breathe deeply and remember it all,
and believe in myself again,
because you saw me
and heard me
and allowed me to be me,
and trusted me
to do the same for you.

I'll remember that we discovered
the space in between,
met there,
and can return to it
any time we need to.

We don't follow each other home

or engage in day to day life.
It doesn't matter to me
if you talk too loudly in restaurants,
or text in a movie theatre,
or whether you bother to use turn signals
when you drive.

These things,
that may frustrate our family and friends,
are suspended here
because none of that matters
to you and me.

What matters is our
willingness
to step into the grey,
into the sacred space
we hold for each other,
and speak the truth.

What matters to us is,
Are you okay?
Do you have what you need to get through today?

I know now
that I can turn to any of you and say,
Help.
Please see me.
Please remind me that I can do this,
and tell me why I must.

My loved ones
can be the reason
I chew with my mouth closed,
but you,

dear recovery friends,
are the reason I live
with my heart open.

Thank you for seeing me.

Thank you for being a mirror
that reminds me
of who I am
and all I can be.

Thank you for your bravery,
for stepping into the place
that others can't acknowledge
to honour your power
and mine.

I am grateful we have chosen to be here.

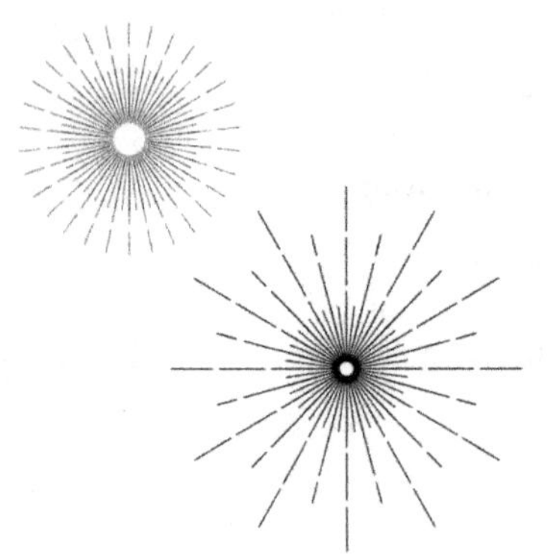

PLEASE DON'T

Please don't play the jester
I do not need to smile
I want to feel my sadness
Just sit with me a while

Please don't play the therapist
Connecting all the dots
Hold space for me and let me share
My darkest fears and thoughts

Please don't play the fixer
With plans to settle scores
Let me vent my anger
Without igniting more

Please don't play the victim
And say you've had it worse
Stories of comparison
Will cause me to reverse

Please stay here beside me
And listen as I speak
Remind me that emotions
Do not make me weak

Please pass the box of tissues
And honour every tear
It's a great relief to shed them
Especially with you near

Thank you for your presence
Your silence through this hour
Not everyone is capable
Of comfort that empowers

SONGS

Songs are but poetry set to music.
These are some favourites
from my days as a performing songwriter.

GRACE

It's so hard, so hard,
Some days, some days
To do what's good.
Oh you want to, want to,
With some help you surely would.

You need a little,
A little of that grace
To get you started,
Get things rolling.
Moves through you,
Gets you going.
You need a little of that grace.

You're doing fine, so fine,
You think, you think that it's alright.
When the road becomes a hill,
Uphill, it's all a fight.
You need a little of that grace.

So keep me running, keep it flowing.
See me laughing, watch me growing.
You see me fail and keep me trying,
Help me reach and hear me crying.
I need a little of your grace.

"Coulee View" Album, 2007

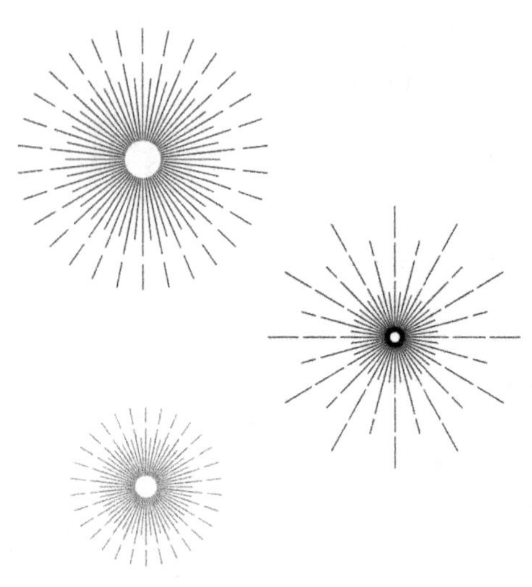

OBLIVION

Oh, they're dropping hints again
But I refuse to let them in
Because I don't want to know
Yeah, it seems the joke's on me
But I don't cry too easily
So it may never show

I'm in oblivion
Sweet oblivion

I have learned to hold my spine
I have learned to speak the lines
That make things okay
I know when to avert my eyes
But I prefer to realize
When it's time to walk away

Back to oblivion
Sweet oblivion

I don't want to hear your truth
I don't need to see your proof
It keeps me from
Oblivion

"Coulee View" Album, 2007

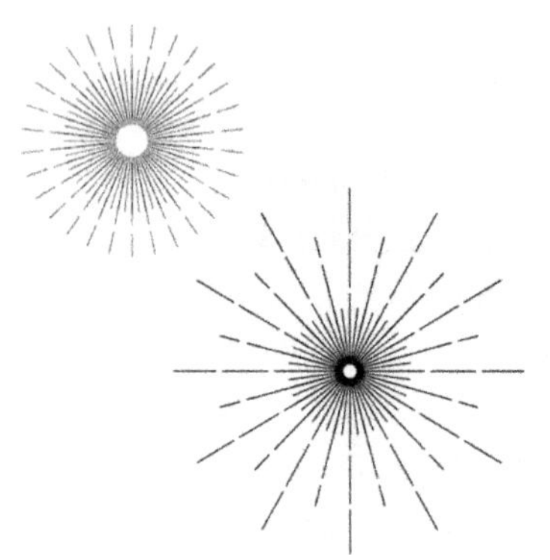

AVOID DANCE

Once I saw you everywhere
Anywhere I'd go.
Now it seems you're never there
In the places you used to like to show.
Must you avoid them altogether now,
These locations I might be?
Is it hard to plan your day
When you're afraid of who you'll see?

I think you thought I knew you knew
All the things you said I said weren't true.
In this web of who is who
I just got tangled up in you.

I saw you betray a friend
With a smile on your face.
Now I watch each word you say
For evidence of falsehood's trace.
Do you see the scrutiny?
Suspect the jig is up with me?
Is that hatred that I see
Or just fermented misery?

Where the angels fear to tread
That's where you lay your head

"Coulee View" Album 2007

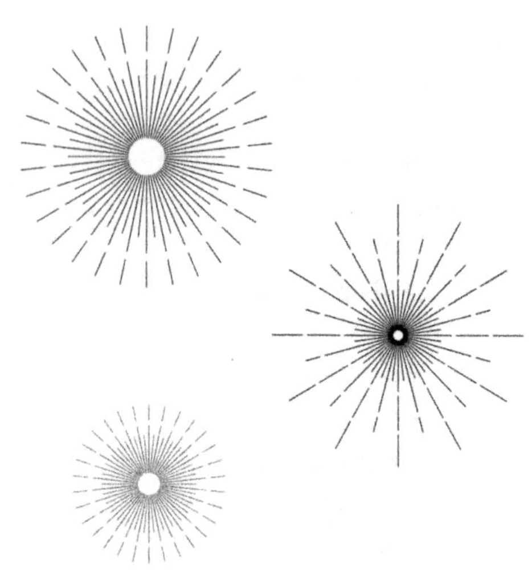

MARY ROSE

One day her mother was headed to town
Came to the stairs and called Mary down
She said, "It's my illness that takes me away,
You're sixteen years now and I'm dying, they say.
So care for the wee ones,
Father needs you this fall.
Mary, you must rise. You've been called."

The following weeks were filled
With sadness and tears
In time Mary took to her tasks with good cheer
She fed them with love,
Sang while mending their clothes
Mary had been called
And she rose.

Mary rose through her sadness
She rose and was strong
She'd be happy again, so she carried along
She held her head high
She was proud just to know
Mary had been called and she rose.
Mary had been called
And she rose.

Later a mother with three of her own
A lonesome decision fell on Mary's new home
The future was frightening but she never froze
Mary felt called and she rose.

Mary rose through her sadness

She rose and was strong
She'd be happy again, so she carried along
She held her head high
She was proud just to know
Mary had been called and she rose.
Mary had been called
And she rose.

Life's filled with pleasures; a garden, a dance,
Family, friends, and sometimes romance
A heart should find joy to soften the scars
The darkest of nights are still filled with stars
Be brave, seek fulfillment, go look for surprise
With all that life gives you should rise.

A graceful dear lady to the end of her days
A sweet disposition, a kind gentle gaze
Surrounded by love, peaceful she glowed
Called one last time, Mary rose.

Mary rose through our sadness
She rose, so be strong
She is happy again so we carry along
Hold your head high and feel proud just to know
Mary was called and she rose.
Mary was called
And she rose.

In loving memory of Mary Campbell
"Coulee View" Album 2007

CONTRAST

All that's relative, all that's true
It's just me trying to see
If I'm still strong next to you

It may seem frivolous and undue
But it's curious to me
How they vanish willingly to be with you

All my courage was growing fast
Up to the line you pushed me past
Where'd my voice go?

All my stars were shining bright
Until you arrived with your blinding light
Where'd the sky go?

All that's relative, all that's true
It's just me trying to see
If I'm still strong next to you

It may seem frivolous and undue
But it's curious to me
How they vanish willingly to be with you

"Blessings and Burdens" Album, 2008

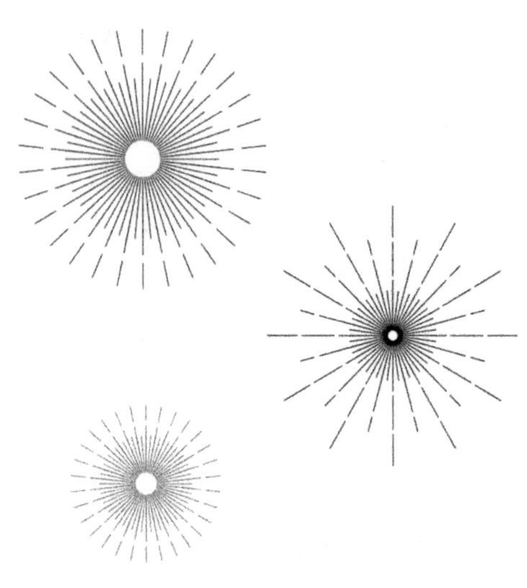

I OWN IT

I own it, I did that
Not proud but that was me
When I face it
I take back a little dignity
I'm not looking for excuses
I just want to be free
From the power weakness had on me

In a darkened corner
Is where shame likes to hide
You think you're strong because
You keep it all inside
It just lays and waits there
To rob you of your pride
Turn the light on, turn the light on
You can shine

You don't have to shout it out
On Main Street to be clear
You don't need to whisper
To confessionary ears
The person you should talk to
Is looking at you in the mirror
And the one who matters most
Can always hear
When you say, "I own it.."
(Free, free, free, free, free....)

"Blessings and Burdens" Album, 2008

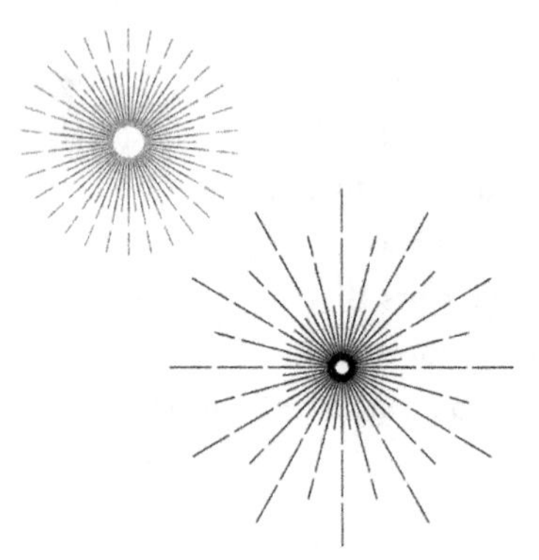

ABOUT THE AUTHOR

Jean McCarthy is a writer and recovery advocate from Alberta, Canada. Her blog "UnPickled" chronicles the ups and downs of life after alcohol. She is the long-time host of "The Bubble Hour" podcast, as well as a novelist and songwriter.

www.jeanmccarthy.ca

ALSO BY JEAN MCCARTHY

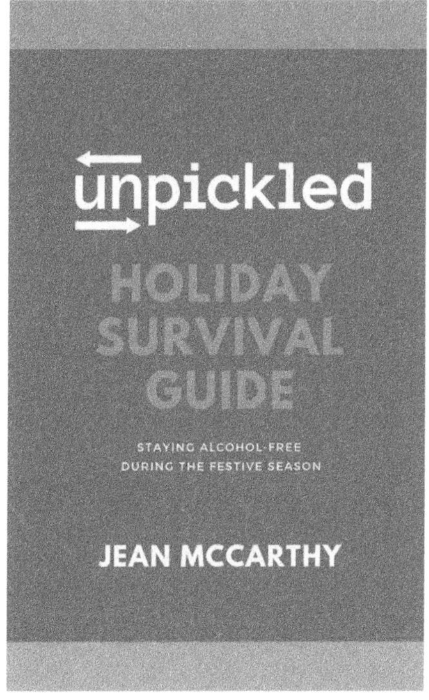

UnPickled Holiday Survival Guide:

Staying Alcohol-Free During the Festive Season

CPSIA information can be obtained
at www.ICGtesting.com
Printed in the USA
BVHW031243200620
581838BV00003B/15

9 781999 299927